Into the Depths:
Exploring The Poetic InnerVerse

Bliss Jones

Copyright © 2022 Rigelle Media Group

Disclaimer

This is a work of fiction. Unless otherwise indicated, all the names, characters, businesses, places, events, and incidents in this book are either the product of the author's imagination or used in a fictitious manner. Any resemblance to actual persons, living or dead, or actual events is purely coincidental.

Published by Rigelle Media Group

Printed in the United States of America
Available online and other retail outlets
First Printing Edition, 2023

Dedication

To my Forever.

Table of Contents

INTRODUCTION

Welcome to my Poetic InnerVerse!

InnerVerse is what I call the universe of my mind or the universe within
The poems I write are about my poetic take.
On my firsthand experiences and experiences of those shared with me.
My style of poetry is more of a poetic storytelling.
This is the second book of the series.
This book delves a little bit deeper into my introverted and sometimes indecisive personality.
As well as looking at how that played out in love and relationships.
I hope you find something that you can connect with, resonate with, or
at the very least find my poetry entertaining,

Thank you for your Purchase!

A Re-introduction

Enigma, Paradox, Anomaly, that's me
Quiet, Innocent looking,
Glasses wearing, Poetry writing Kee

There's there the alter ego
The quiet girl's She-ro
She says and does all the things
Kee would never say or do
It used to be hard to correlate the two
Especially being raised w/there's certain things good girls just don't do

Yet the catalyst that birthed Torrential Bliss's induction
Said there's no need for the character reduction
What I have is the perfect seduction
A blending of the shy & nerdy Lady in the streets
& the complete make a dick disappear type of freak, in the sheets

I used to need full acceptance
Someone gave me that
Saw the good, bad, and ugly
He never stepped back
I ran and I ducked
He never veered off track
Desired mental stimulation
Gave that…and feedback
Fucked around and gave him my heart
That, humph, he never gave back

As I get older & embrace maturity
I'm more patient & kind
No more insecurity
My inner confidence shines
More importantly,
I enjoy who I am
Torrential Bliss has arrived
and she's integrated fully in
Ppl have their opinions but,
I respectfully… don't give a damn.
Take me or leave me
For I am who I am

Part Two

The woman standing before you,
is brand new
A more evolved version,
Not just the girl you knew.
Back when we were 26 & 22
Time passed.
I did what I did
& you'd do what you do
There were times when we allowed the other to come through
Yet, Life, achievements, disappointments, experiences, interesting choices &
mistakes
Are all apart of reasons we grew.

& I'm eagerly interested in learning the new parts of you.
Looking forward to your take on the things you been through
& Regardless of the changes in life the constant, in my heart was you.
Sometimes the creator allows us a glimpse of our destiny
Then sends us on a path to where we need to be.
It appears things are stripped or taken away but in reality,
All this was cause for this….
we weren't really ready.

Thinking we were grown.
Yet swimming in immaturity
Misconceived notions of loyalty, fidelity, & security.
So, we end up dimming our own light to feel another's love.
When in all actuality it was us, they were unworthy of
Hiding perceived darkness so others cannot see.
Yet true love, humph, it accepts totally
Growing together but respecting individuality.
I want to see your darkness
Inspire my kinky
Show me all of you,
As I stand before you nakedly

See the pain we felt
When we thought we fumbled the bag,
And the feeling of loss,
When we thought we lost all we had
Our perceived trials by fire were our crosses to bear.
Yet these tribulations were actually just preparation
A misunderstood gestation
Birthing new versions of us

Through what we thought as the worse dilation
What we been through,
Taught us the end is being committed
To someone not committed to learning you.

Conceit

This poem will be completely centered around me!
Yes! I'm choosing Today,
To celebrate my conceit!
I know, I know,
I come across all mild and meek
Yet my personality ranges from Crazy to Zen
Yet when it comes to my Poetic pen
I stand up here as an Empress among men
My intellect is on fleek
I may not be your particular taste
But I ADORE ME!

I've been called nerdy, quiet, bitchy and stuck up
Yet, none of those titles bother me
Because I Do Not Give a Fuck!
For far too many years I worried about what other people may think.
Other's opinions laying in my mind like indelible ink.
Self-consciousness put me in a shell
So, from others eyes I would shrink.
I'm betting that was the basis of my stage fright, I think

Being hated on cause
You don't see what I see
Or hating because you don't love you...
Like I love me
Yet here I am all setbacks, obstacles,
& Salt thrown overcame.
 Beautifully I stand here
No shame in my game
So deep is my conceit
I need two goddamn names!
I mean I am Bliss Jones
& It's not just a stage name
Yet, Torrential Bliss
Is a description of how my love rains
& If you've ever experienced me.

Unconventional

Unconditional is what it is
Not situational
Or relational
So, despite what we've been through
It is what it is

When we were younger His eye I caught
As we matured, lessons were taught
We've both lived life.
Entertaining others
His time, or attention not sought
Throughout it all, I held a piece of his heart.

Although…
Unknowingly so…
I was unaware
I didn't see the signs
When I did.
I attributed it to something else
So, I paid it no-never-mind

So, I never put on airs.
Never tried to impress
Friends…
Regardless of everything else,
Never felt a need to obsess
or possess
Nor finesse

I know what's between
My ears, my legs
& up under my breasts
Unlike others,
Even if I felt it,
Never acted like,
Or showed I was pressed
Named me Orgasmic Bliss
If I called… He came
Like a man possessed
All this before Bliss Jones became the name
I'm the owner,

Of the house on the hill in his brain.

An Enigma,
No drama,
A breath of fresh air, that's me
Cool conversation,
Beauty,
& Sensuality
Open minded, Intelligent
With a flair for Originality
Tradition has its place
Yet, I represent…Unconventionality

A mix of the past,
A touch of the new.
I promise NO ONE ELSE…
Gets the reactions I do.
I promise, I left a mark
Feel sorry if he's now with you.
Once unconventional has been tasted
A traditional wife,
or relationship just won't do.

School of You

Like an advertisement,
I've seen you around a time or two
Won't lie Interest piqued
Plus noticing a bit of chemistry too.
Respectful vibe.
Attention given, Yet not an open pursuit.
Interestingly,
Not letting my influence overtake you.
Your Energy indirectly placed,
In my field of view.
Curiosity awakened....,
I think I might want to enroll
In the school of you.

You get to play teacher
As your student,
I'll tentatively submit to you
Show me what you know.
I wanna learn how you do.
What are your interests?
What do you like?
Are there others in this school?
If there are, just know no cutting corners
I like to win, but within the rules
Leaving your former valedictorian
Confused & looking like a fool.

I'll shoot to the head of the class.
Well known as a nerd.
So, there's no doubt I'll pass.
Others, humph, they do their best
Due diligence done,
Assignments understood
Other spots I divest
With my mental proficiency, It's nothing,
for me to pass your tests.
Even in Home Ec....

Others may know
of your preferred flavors.
Yet you've yet to taste my zest.

My scrumptiousness melts in your mouth.
Once you imbibe my nectar
you'll know why I'm the best
From stranger to star pupil
Let me formally introduce myself.
I am Torrential Bliss,
& with my bliss you'll be blessed.

Tied Souls

I'm avoidant
You handle things anxiously
I run.
You apologize
Yet, never fully letting go of me
Like a spirit
I'm always with you & You're with me
Tried cleansing baths & cutting cords
That shit…wouldn't stick.
Learned emotional isolation,
While in the thick of it.
Emotions like an ocean
The depths so deep
Yet, You…swim…within…expertly
When we're apart
We're in each other's heart….
& head
If you dare to move on
The others feel the memories of me,
In your bed
Outside Relationships, like The Walking Dead

Souls tied

Like a catalyst your logic helped me grow
I went from the shy girl
To your girl
Now that's all I know
Came out of my shell
Parts kept within, I now show
Through my Inhibitions,
& sometimes boundaries you'd plough
Even without hands
This connection, we've yet to really let go
From lessons to pain,
To pleasures, that left me aglow.
Without your prompting
The world wouldn't even see this poetic flow

Souls tied

Both our hearts fragile
Yet it's me, your soul craves
You don't have to admit, I know
I feel it & feel the same way.
May or may not comment but…
I see your love displays
Yet this version of love…,
I don't know, atypical &
Hits in a completely different way
Not bound by kids or contracts
Never needed to trap or….
Obligate you to stay
Even when you're not physically next to me
You're with me always

Souls tied

Forever my love
Forever my friend
Doesn't even matter,
What dimension we're in
In the Spiritual, Astral & Physical too
At times when we physically connect,
All these realms I go through.
Respect given freely
No desire to change you
I love who you are.
The only man I bow too

Souls tied

Struck and captivated by our intensity!
By our chemistry,
Empathy,
Transparency,
Understanding & Clarity,
Even…our Sincerity
Not to mention the Ecstasy
When we're together it all just flows…effortlessly…
Plus, The lengths you go through,
Just to See Me
Loving you, whether together, or apart, endlessly.

Souls Tied

Midnight Sun

My battery sometimes gets low.
As the day winds down
I'm even walking slow
Somewhere along the path of my day,
& Being helpful to others,
I inadvertently lost my glow.
I get home & I'm tired don't feel like doing….
a thing, but shower & sleep.
I don't even eat, don't have the energy
So, Shower to cleanse the day off of me
& Sleep for rest, growth, & subtle recharging

Then, unexpectedly, came you.
Divine design is well thought through
We humans want to make other humans think…
We Know more than we actually do.
Yet….
It's like God created a rapid charger for me
Within you
There's electricity in your touch.
The simple act of an embrace,
I never realized I needed so much.

Wait a minute, let me explain.
& for that, I have to back up….
Your voice…
the very first thing to attract me to you.
It intrigued me.
Your melodic tempo caused my interests to accrue
Your face then caught me too
Excitement, but no butterflies
It's had the calming effect of,
watching the roll of an ocean tide go from white, crashing back into blue.
The words out of your mouth gave me a glimpse inside your mind.
Your Intelligence pulled me in
Like others attraction to your being Fine.
& Yes, you are fine.
& It was noticed too
Yet pain sometimes comes wrapped in your preferences
So, physical features I've learned to see,
& Look through.

It was your word formulation,
That Birthed in me, the temptation
That drew me to you.
See, I'd been craving mental stimulation
So, the conversations with other guys, from that moment,
reached a point of cessation.
I didn't need to get my ass wet because,
Our conversation…
gave me a different level of elation.
You listened & actually retained & understood,
This to me was a friendship foundation.
& I knew…. we would be good.
I didn't see the design
or what was being done.
I didn't see that you were ultimately sent,
I didn't see that you were the one.
I did not see you could bring me to
Orgiastic levels without physically making me cum.
I did not realize when I'm mentally drained and need to be alone,
I could be with you & still charge.
You are…like the paradox of a midnight sun.

So, the mental is taken care of
 and the emotional too.
Let's just say you make me feel seen and I do my best to see you.
Then there's the physical.
Yet it's more like astrophysical mixed with metaphysical.
The lengths & realms I'm brought to, (sigh) seems…almost nonsensical.
Yet the divine gave me this poetic flow to translate how I feel
& help others comprehend the incomprehensible.

Socks

When I stopped searching
I found you, or better yet, you found me.
I'd stop searching so....
Though it was in front my face, I did not see
Plus, the packaging I expected,
Was arranged differently.
I was looking for tall, dark, and handsome
Yet...you came wrapped... handsomely.
Though the Chocolate was milk, not dark.
& I didn't have to look up.
Because you were at eye level with me.
I should have known from my grandparents
Sometimes your perfect match,
May not match conventionality.
Like....I love art.
& Maybe, that's why you're covered in tattoos.
Art was something ALL my past loves would do.
Sketching, painting & a singer too.
The creator is really funny too. Humph.,
Because...The art isn't what you do,
The Art is Simply You!

So, A series of events turned us into lovers
Then back to friends.
& A secondary series turned the clock back again.
Tired of the merry go round.
I decided to stop, choosing the end.
Love ain't supposed to be this hard,
I thought.

This ain't the reason I went through bullshit
This ain't the reason why I fought.
Through the pain, my own heart I'll mend.
Though broken ties weren't severed clean.
& I learned to silence my internal screams.
My fumbled heart was mended,
Yet it's stronger, with these beautiful scars it seemed.
As the world kept spinning another series of events brought me back to you.
Older, but, his time double the complications we went through.
Well, I did. I don't know about you.
Then again, I think you had your own complications to attend to.

One of your girls commented on ties not being severed clean, being a thing....
I started thinking maybe he wasn't my match but a vehicle that came to bring
karma through.
I meditate. (Deep sigh)
We are on this planet to learn....
So, this time let me take it slow.
Nom yo ho reng ge key oh.
So maybe these experiences are what's needed for my soul to grow.

Regardless of whatever we remain friends
With or without sex.
Establishing permanence
No kids play, but we're friends to the end
The problem is, I wanna spin the block again.
I think I'm addicted
I want to feel you again.
I now need a series of events,
In my life, just so I can be free.
I want it again, but this time I want it. differently
I wanna show off my swimming skills.
I wanna dive deep. No surface level shit
I want to snorkel in your energy.
You were never hidden
Yet I now want you openly.
No drama or intrigues, just...simplicity
My outlook changed after reaching maturity
Like Monica, I want your love, all over me.
I want to rub on your back
and kiss all over your face.
I want you to build houses and live inside
my internal space.
I know that time has passed but...
 I can give you babies metaphorically.
White paintballs all over my walls...
It's cool...
They'll be cleansed with Niagara-like falls.
I'm longer vanilla, more like strawberry
Mentally covering my face....
because even poetically,
This.... brings the shyness out of me.
Although.... I enjoy...
Being your favorite type of freak.
Shit I didn't even know was inside,
You're bringing out of me.

I'm no longer trying to keep it inside.
I express it all openly
I even bought new socks
So, we can go back to the beginning,
& Again, you can knock them off of me.

Breakthrough

I am coming up on a pinnacle.
Currently in an upslope.
Yet, those that seen me in my darkest
May have described me as cynical
I've never been one that came across as whimsical.
More commonly known as quiet & analytical.
Always helpful to others,
Yet me seeking help was… atypical.

They say a closed mouth don't get fed.
& Since I kept my mouth closed.
I suffered malnutrition & damn near ended up dead.
Yet this process of Life, love, pain, death, and rebirth.
Gave me experiences that hit home like
Something akin to God's daily bread.

I had a breakthrough
Anxiety & Fear had Walls talking
I felt like I was in a mental prison
Wrists slit to let out life
Yet the creator closed that incision.
Was told yeah you have free will,
Yet, the endpoint is not your decision.
Pain, blocked my comprehension
So…The divine, gave me a vision
I was looking elsewhere
Yet in me, he, she, and they were risen.
I couldn't quit. I had shit to do.
I was specifically created,
For these things to be done through.

Yes…. I am…coming up on a pinnacle.
This dark night; my mind, body, & soul went through
Gave me something critical…
Shit I Never knew I needed
The process was alchemical.
I… am… now… transformed.
Jewels no longer hidden in my heart.
My crown, hand, and wrist are now properly adorned.

Shit…This light I have. Is for all to see.

Fuck that shy girl shit.
I am not here, just for me!
Bible thumpers don't clutch your pearls Despite my language, I know you feel me.
It took a few decades for me to even properly process my own energy.
So, when I come through
 I know it's me you see.
Hell, I had to apologize to myself, for sleeping on the true version of me.
Yet my purpose is not to come and show anyone up.
I know I have haters but I really don't give a fuck
I'm simple, not flashy
A lil hood remains but I'm classy

Yet I was sent, to let the world bask…
 in my ambient glow.
& The story of my journey
may even help you grow.
& sometimes share a lil bit of my poetic flow.
This breakthrough brought me what I needed to see
To rise to out of the depths, I was in
To higher levels of frequencies
Yet, if I have knowledge you need,
Just ask and I'll bestow.
We all need a lil help sometimes to up our personal tempo.

She is Me

You decide to come at me,
Yet I respond… silently,
You're following my socials
Trying to see what I do.
Wondering is there anything in me,
That you can see in you
You said, he said, I'm just a friend
Yet…. y'all have yet to say I do.
You're trying to find out who is she….
Well,….. I'll help you.
I am her and she is me.

They say the energy of lovemaking melts
Into the skin.
Even if he showered.
Bitch, I'm still all over him
I'm permanent, like the ink of the tattoos in his skin.
Even in your bed…
When he moans in his sleep
He's dreaming of fucking me.
I do not need your spot, baby
Like Donell Jones
Where I'm at, is where he wants to be.
That ghost in your relationship
I am her & she is me

You & I, we both know he loves to swim
& Believe me Chile, when I say
He gets his strokes in.
From his private pool where only he,
had a key
Or better yet his personal private jacuzzi
Warm and wet as can be.
No need for him to prepare
He's always ready for me.
No need to use Vaseline over here
to front like I'm juicy
Like a clairvoyant, let me tell you what I see.
You were chosen babe because I was not free
Still trying to figure out who I am?
Well…I am her & she is me

Chile, I can't even remember
The last time we were together sexually.
Ask him though,
I bet he remembers.
You may be his current reality
But I am his fucking ultimate fantasy.
When you see him licking his lips.
You can bet he's remembering the taste of me.
Apologies though,
For being the source of your insecurity.
He's your man but…
No
One
Else
Compares to me.
Humph,
I'm apart of his mentality
You can't get rid of even the memory of me
Meanwhile I'm over here living my life happily.
Unfortunately for you, his heart is with me, spiritually
& Babee, I don't even have to be there physically.
Because I am Her and She is Me!

You call me a side chick, humph
Supposedly, I want your life
Chile please…..
Nobody over here wants all your stress and your strife.
No apologies because you came looking for me,
You woke the sleeping beast
Not my fault you living with my ghostly presence
and I'm not even deceased.
Ghetto gagging, ass munching, fake ass sanctified, forever girlfriend, my bad,
fiancé
Holding down his kid
Cause he gave you his nutt,
Not his last name.
& You thinking I'm over here wanting to do the same.
Worrying about where "my man" is?
and what it is "my man" do?
I'll let you in on a secret.
I was here, in his head, way before you.

& You wonder why
My name keeps popping up like it do,
You can try to replace me.
As a matter of fact...
I DARE You!
When the dust settles,
HERE, I WILL BE!
& Do You know why?
Because I am her
 & She is Me!

Vacancy

Everyone that knows me says that I'm real.
Is the real deal.
 Look, I been holding this shit in
But fuck it, the beans need to be spilled.
I have a vacancy over here.
& I need to have it immediately filled.

I have heard there is a declining level of applicant quality.
I'm feeling like what the fuck that got to do with me?
I do not need quantity
Hell & there are very few that actually even attract me.
Plus, I have an exceptional eye
And there's myriad of things that will disqualify.
I need a very particular type of guy
That's why the last position holder had to say bye.

I'm told that I'm finicky
Yet not many have what it takes to satisfy me
Hell, to even get the show started honestly.
I need someone who can match,
or exceed me, mentally.
Show an unfamiliar perspective from what I normally see.
Do you have a life plan?
Do you know how to lead?
Ambitious?
Somewhat materialistic,
but not to the point of greed?

Are you authoritative?
Can I look up to you?
Are you intelligent?
What's your IQ
Can you teach me?
That is what's required, to experience….my freaky.
That is what's required, for me to respond…softly and submissively

Will you metaphorically lick
the crevices of my brain.
Intellectually drive my lady parts insane.
Cum inside my thoughts…
& Bring a smile to my face

Have me excited,
to mold my lips around your name.
Have me talking to spirits about how hard I came.

Before all this,
make sure, you're sure, about me.
Because…
All this is before…experiencing my body
All this is before…equipment inspections you see.
I'm going through these lengths,
because I require permanency.
All this, is before being invited to fill,
my vaginal vacancy.

Superstar

Bend over you say…
Hmm…. I like your boldness, poetic dialect
& verbal wordplay
It seems we've come to this point of…
What Aunt Shirley Say,
Lol……As we lay
You said enough is enough
It seems I've awakened the semi silent beast
And for me, on my body you aim to feast.

Cool cool…. But soul possession?
My dear sir, you got me fucked up
If you think from sucking on my juices
My soul I'll give up.
Jealousy…even in 25 different languages
Nah, sir, That Ain't me!
But I promise even if I lay there and do nothing, when it's done
A new level of sunshine you'll see!
You should have left me alone,
While I was sitting there quietly.

No need to be my Jay.
& No need for me to be you your Bey
My Bae's at home anyway
& I am Rejecting your lyrical foreplay
Yet, I promise,
I'm showing you a level of modesty
& Definitely restraint,
Of humbleness
& Of humility
When I say, if I gave you a taste
You'd be my groupie.
Like a superstar,
Fighting through a line of suitors surrounding me.
Not understanding
When I do play these games,
I play for keeps
But warning, my juices laced
with something akin to heroin
One taste and you're addicted
No need for penetration

Fuck...remembered!
Me.... you will forever crave!
Have you dropping all your bitches
So me, you can satiate,
This craving, that at the mention of my name,
Makes you salivate.
That beast that was awakened,
Sir, you might wanna put his ass,
Back to sleep, before he's conquered,
& He chooses... to belong to me.

Boundaries

The fondest of memories for the girl I used to be.
The day we met, changed my entire trajectory.
Released were the fears, hidden within me.
I asked how did you know?
No one else could see.
You said you didn't know.
Your only aim was to please.
The pleasure you brought changed previous boundaries.

Nothing over here with us is bland.
Taboos explored
Regrets abandoned
My specific kink, besides praise
I love it when u give commands
Even better with no words
Just…directed with your hands
Show me where u want me to go
Tell me what u want me to do
My boundaries are…
I only submit to you.

Private Affair

Over here preparing to do my thing.
As you walk in.
Although you said you'd be here
Won't lie, I'm surprised, yet again
I'm looking at my audience
Wondering do they feel the heat…
The rise… in the temperature
From you simply walking in the building.
Do they feel the vibration,
Of my temptation,
Or maybe this inner elation,
From the anticipation of tonight's future sin.

Our interactions, they fuel my glow
Ur smile, is that Spanish fly, to ignite
The sparks that become an inferno.
It's a turn on because how we get down….
No one really knows
I've Past issues with
Going public
then out, come the storytelling hoe's
With the oh girl we used to mess around
Or he's a dog, you need to send his ass back to the pound.
Your too good for him,
Or He tried to holler at me
A different story for every day
So, I adjust to dating in private, being my way
Yet the way you lick & nibble on my lips,
Gives amnesia, to my directional flow.
Even if I wanted to leave,
I wouldn't know which way to go.
U catch my eye, smile, and lick your lips.
I'm thinking umph really tho…

Although, I am private,
& You were never hidden.
Yet, unknown to the world are our intentions.
Because well…,
I don't like people in my business
A few…know what's up
Some see us as friends.

Most don't know we even know each other
Cause in Kenner we're from different ends
Yet…. your presences adds to the show
A bit of…. sexual tension.
Even…. if your name is never mentioned,

Intellect tapped & behind closed doors
Ur Ass gripped, mine smacked
Our softer parts gently kissed
sometimes before we part….
you're already missed.
Whether or not your known
Other niggas…..quickly dismissed
I got what u want
You got what I need
Long as we're good
Fuck keeping the world up to speed.

Not confirmed or denied
Yet passion's now hard to subdue
Soooo after I do, what I do
After you hear, what I say
After you feel, my poetic prose
& taste, the ambiance I lay.
I'm curious about your reaction
To seeing my emotion on display
It's seems I'm now truly ready to go all in
& The veil between public & private's
it's becoming real thin.

In & Out

You got me to open
Got me to let guards down
Got me to let you in
No, I'm not talking days, weeks, or months,
I mean, years of leg work put in
Maybe, I took too long…
Maybe, you got tired of waiting
Then again, in the very beginning…
I was, all in
My feelings weren't quite there but…
I was, at the very least, open.
Then You…pumped the brakes.
I tried, but couldn't forget
So, no matter what, out, in my brain,
Those words would stick
Even when you pleaded to come back.
We were moving too fast,
Is what you said you meant
Misconstrued words
& Confused intent
You wanted to slow things a bit,
Not bring about our end,

Allowed back in,
Because...My Discernment was skewed
Never before have my Innards,
Walls & boundaries been moved
Yet, to the depth of feelings shown,
There was NOW a limit.
Even though standing on a cliff,
Allowing myself to fall,
became something to prohibit
Yet, I still can't say what you did, and didn't feel
Continuously my mind's repeatedly replaying shit,
I'm trying to remember what was really really real.

I never really was one to pay attention to the details
Yet with you, an analyst, I became,
and all that entails.
Cause lord knows I'm extra and…
I be going all off the rails

Yet for you, no matter how I fought it,
Those pesky feelings, once they grew, seemed to always prevail.
My trust even reached a point that I didn't even give a fuck, about other females
& When it comes to other guys,
Child please ain't no comparison,
Once you're placed on the fuckin scales.
Other men don't stand a chance,
Guy friends playing the long game,
trying to get me under their spell
Disappearing cause once they lay eyes on you…, Humph
Just your presence…gives em' fucking hell
Then again, Fuck them scales,
You Are, the entire fucking pedestal.
In my head…Totally & Completely, set apart
No matter how many times I walked away
My silly ass repeatedly gave you my heart.

I gave it to you so many times.
My chest no longer felt like it's home
If not in your presence I could only find emotic rest inside the lines of a poem
I walk away……You chase
So I'd fade into the background
Hoping you wouldn't notice,
So, my emotions could have a bit of space
Yet when you feel like toying with me again
Once again my dumb ass heart
Like a revolving door,
Let's you right back on in
It's to the point, I can't even rely on my friends
They know it's a cycle
They be like here she go merry-go-rounding again.
I'm good all alone then,
Then, you simply say Hi
I completely melt,
Simply knowing you want me again
& Remembering how you intoxicated all of my senses,
Your sound,
your smell,
your taste,
Even the sight of you…Captivates
& then feeling of…mmm, the penetration,
The expansion of my ramparts
To fit the girth of our particular sin.
Remembering how orgasms,

brought ethereal explosions & out of body experiences!
If I didn't already have kids
I'd have taken our first time for an expertly executed deflowering demo
& The last time…. Could have been mis-taken for a waterworks show.
The way, storms flowed from my eyes and repeated Tsunami waves from below…

I try to chill, knowing…. I shouldn't let you back in
& On a couple of occasions,
you've committed offenses
That was grounds for impeachment or immediate termination.
Yet, my heart overtakes my brain.
Your proximity brings heart palpitations.
Over here thinking, why would God do this to me?
I know I shouldn't question it.
It's the Right place, right time,
& the answer is right before me.
Yet it is lost to me,
I'm discombobulated,
Using my eyes to hear & my ears to see.
Perplexed because I fear our particular intensity.
My femininity is completely receptive to your all of your masculine energy.
Exposed humanity, & my heart's inherent frailty
This predicament is because with you,
I have a lack of boundaries.
When physically connected it's hard to discern
the beginning of you & the ending of me.
Manifestation of a 5D circle of spherical chi

No more in & out,
Yet, this decision has always lain with me.
Either go all In or ……go all out
& Walk away fully.
They say always to thine own heart be true.
If I'm really honest.
I find my peace when with you.
Since you're my choice.
The decision has been made,
Now what do I do?

Commitment

I fell ass backward into a commitment.
I didn't know what I was doing.
I was busy minding my business.
I had college, a couple of kids and a job to maintain.
I had no intentions on playing with nobody not trying to change
 My fucking last name.
But….it had been while.
After all the calls, texts, & time spent,
He seemed cool.
I told myself fuck it; I oughta let him knock the cobwebs loose.
You know a lil maintenance fuck
I had heard I was repressed
Let's see, if he, could loosen me up

I fell ass backwards into a commitment
Man. Look. He cleared the cobwebs with just his tongue.
I passed out, was limp…My body went dead.
Then this Nigga resurrected me…
by Not, stopping the head.
Orgasms, brought me back dead
Is this nigga Black Jesus?
Did he just present me with Lazarus head?
Then he brought out ALL This Dick
that had me Thanking god & calling Gwen cause….
I just knew he was the one.
When he penetrated…..
I thought I saw glory.
I'm thinking oh shit, this right here, this is it!
My heart stopped
I was transported to a place where I saw
blue skies, green grass & shining ones on the mount.
Don't know what the fuck that was but
Yea this here is the end of my self-imposed drought
Too many times we went to this place between time and space
Where we left our bodies and were just merging energies
 Orbited by cosmic clouds in our own personal innerspace.

I told y'all I fell ass backwards into commitment.
He had me in awe,
The color of my life now shaded by his tint.
I swear on my cervix nigga left an imprint

Even we disconnect I could feel his energy.
Yet to him this was completely foreign
He contemplated it all silently
as I shared the places he catapulted me to
Hmmm, his silence made me think I was alone, or crazy, or worse…
I thought was this just regular to you?
So, it's just sex? It was nothing profound?
I know for a fact, there aren't others like me floating around.
but I waited
because to me, this here was meant.
Even without sex the energy would still get me bent
Then after a while it seemed, all was wasted &The time that we spent.

I fell ass backwards into a commitment
See I learned in hindsight we weren't rooted in reality.
It wasn't all on him
Some of the blame falls on me.
There we're some really good things,
Like him seeing my beauty
& Helping to release that shyness from me.
Though, I never did get that new last name
Or a forever consolation prize.
I did learn that Omission equals,
the same as lies
& His love may have ran its course
Or maybe it was lust in disguise.
Yet, When it was over….
After the initial darkness left
Then came the eventual…sunrise.
I felt its warmth and it didn't feel glorious initially
I've now been immersed in the light and the dark.
With divine help I've found the capacity to overcome it all
& it was all encased within me.
I fell ass backwards into commitment,
 but I was alone & true commitment didn't find me.
I am however…
wiser & grateful for the lessons & experiences…
bestowed upon me.

Safe Space

So much going on in the world
Media lies, war and inflation
It even trickles down to family connections
& broken relations
Between real and fake
It's hard to find filtration
What's good and bad depends on
The perspective of what we see
What's good to others
Isn't necessarily what's good to me
That's why my safe space
is right here, with just me

Don't have time for manipulation and deceit
Misconstrued stories people tell
Giving the potatoes with no meat.
Lies being offered, told on repeat
BS received as truth by drunkards and dummies
Sometimes storytellers themselves don't remember the real story.
Well, At least….Not honestly
Looking like fools when the story is told
In front of people who were really there to see.
Intelligence insulted, by fallacy
Claiming mental superiority
99.9% isn't the same…
As 0% You should be ashamed.
That's why my safe space is here,
Alone with just me

Then my supposed inner circle,
My friends, lovers, my family
The ones whom were let inside my shell
The ones I let really see….me
The ones with whom I shared my vulnerabilities
Nurture not nature, caused this version of me
Feeling like an island in a violent sea
Not realizing my placement was
Intervention by divinity.
To become omniscient, you have to experience invisibility
That's why my safe space is here
Alone with just me.

On my island which I left unexplored
Was everything needed,
A smorgasbord
Even Sparsely populated with others on one accord.
Past experiences are what prepared me
To see my inner nobility.
Leaving behind people and places that no longer served me.
Some arrived on their own journey.
It seemed my path, not the island, was just for me
An island named Maturity
Forgiveness doesn't require continued access you see.
Even in maturity, my safe space is still
Alone with just me.

Comfortable being on my own
Confident in my decisions alone
Not needed was others to lean on.
So imagine my surprise when I realized
Another was in my home.
...I didn't trust it. Who sent you?
Is my safe space, even large enough for two?
How do I know your really safe?
How do I know you won't hurt me too?
Intrigued though, I allow you to stay,
but over there.... is for you.
You gently invaded my space.
Now its colored with you
Intoxicated by your scent
I instinctually, bow to you
Didn't even notice...
You softly took down some walls too
Space rearranged, what did you do?
Having everything I need now, includes you.
& When you touch me....hmmm
......Electricity....Whoo
Still alone in my safe space
But now alone is us two.

Deed Completed

Half sleep
Your dick on my ass
Your hand on my hips
You're still fully sleep
You don't even feel this
I arch my back
So maybe you can feel I want more
You're still sleeping
Silence interrupted by the cutest little snore
Ego deflated, I wanna let you sleep
But...my body wants more...

So, I turn to face you
Like a weirdo, I love watching you sleep
No matter the circumstance
Something about, seeing you at peace
Feeling special
Cause it's shared with me
There's strength in shared vulnerabilities
Closer I get, as I kiss on your chest
Still nothing
Thinking Damn I might need to chill
& Let this man get his rest
I tell myself; I'll wait til he's awake
Then how I feel, I can express
So for now (Deep sigh)
My desire I suppress

I resist the urge to touch myself
He always tells me I think too much
In the very beginning, He described it as...
Me being repressed and such
Writing, is how I let what's in my head out
But fuck all that, I put his dick in my mouth
But with all that I do
I don't just give head...
Its more like giving throat
Don't let these glasses fool you
I hold the title,
I'm the GOAT
Fuck all modesty

On this imma gloat.

Believe me when I say I go all out for mine
Skills like this,
You don't hear about them in the streets
If a dude ever had me
I promise you, a chord was struck
Oh, I left a memory.
But back to my dude,
Cause now he's fully awake
Taking him all in
Like a naughty nurse
I'm using his dick, to intubate
What he got inside
Is what my body needs
What I got inside needs to be released

But he stops me,
He wants me to ride ... hmm (devilish smile)
He wants to cum inside
I sit on it,
I love doing what I'm told
I cum immediately
I feel him watching me
As I tremble & my eyes roll
He pulls me close,
Fucking the shit out of me
In my ear he says
Right now! Cream all over this dick.
My rhythm matches his as I do what I do
My walls squeezing him
As I moan I love you.
He groans and says oh shit
As he cums too

I don't move
I don't like the disconnection
I leave him inside
til he fully loses his erection
I then lay back in his arms,
As all energy has been depleted
We fall back to sleep
As the deed has been completed.

Alone

We had a time and it was fun
Getting to know each other
Watching the years go and come.
Remembering the time just being in your company my heart would beat
Like a bass drum
Who…. would have known the outcome
My love for you was as deep as can be
At times I believe, I loved you more than me
Feeling your touch gave me 9 different levels of happy
You brought friendship, pleasure, passion and ecstasy more importantly you
stimulated me mentally

Never imagined I would one day feel this way
Never imagined I would one day have these words to say
Never imagined my welcome I'd outstay
Watching this illusion of a relationship crumble and decay.
Never did I imagine one day, I would walk away.

So in love, I watched the changes In you
So in love, I let you do what you do
So in love, I continue to show up….
& with a broken heart too
So in love, I couldn't imagine life without you

I would lie in the dark not wanting to see the light
I would lie in the dark, fuck fight or flight
I would lie in dark tears in my ears
& Sad lyrics I'd recite
I would lie in the dark praying love would be finite
I would lie in the dark hoping for perpetual night

Yet like always the morning did come
and the sun did arise
I'm a big girl
& the truth was surmised
Eventually able to go cold turkey on the addiction of having you inside.
Eventually seeing some of my choices…
were probably unwise
Eventually, I acted my age & swallowed my pride.
Eventually threw on my heels & adjusted my stride.

Love isn't finite, when it's true
Yet loving someone doesn't require attachment or tethering to
So, fully in love, I walked away from you.
Believing if it was meant to be
Love never really dies
Some how
Some way,
Someday,
You will return to me.
Yet, Being alone….
Hardest shit I ever had to do.
Yet, I became the center of my own innerverse
Not you
A friend once told me sometimes you have to
Leave the one you love
To find the one that loves you.

Currency

Lying here…
feeling the ache of feeling all alone.
It's crazy because I'm secure
I'm lying here in my bed,
here in my own home.
Not worried bout bills
I got a man that will do anything for me.
Doesn't know how but desires to bring the soft life to me.
Yet communication & comprehension is like foreign currency
We don't fully understand each other yet we know that currency is needed to make
the waters flow
So just above the bare minimum is done just to keep shit afloat.
If we don't sink, I can't see
That he lacks swimming skills (he thinks) &
I can't see that his lack of navigation's real (he thinks)
He's thinking what he does should make me happy.
I'm observant & He claims to be clairvoyant
All the while he's married to a woman he can't even clearly see.
He sees the brains, my heart & my loyalty
Sometimes I believe my beauty,
he sees it even more than me
Yet, He says he understands the substance underneath
There is past pain & trauma I'm healing so to my children I don't bequeath.
My language is ancient
He gets key words but I doubt his fluency.
Similar words ain't always got the same etymology.
If you can't clearly read my metrics
how are you fully understanding me?
That's why communication & comprehension, to me,
Is true currency.
Then to move to the exchange of energy.
A lot of the time I feel drained like I'm running on empty.
Only you are fulfilled in our sexual synergy,
Like I'm carrying dollars & you have yen.
I'm spending energy
But it's not cycled back in.
Yet I'm still required to spend.
So, I gotta figure out another way to
Replenish the storage with in.
Yet it's frowned upon to bring another banker in.
Any outside influence is considered competition.

Therapist needed for an intervention.
Considering dissension.
Was taught energy exchange is supposed to be the glue.
Well, the glue don't stick & the currency ain't thick.
So, what am I supposed to do?
Even without speaking the same language
I know you feel it too.
I'm told everyone meets for a reason
A lesson or blessin
Well maybe growth & awareness was the reason
Maybe…we weren't for a lifetime, but a season.

FWB (Friends with Benefits)

I don't want a husband or a boyfriend
I have businesses and responsibilities
So, I don't have that much time to spend
I don't need someone trying to control my free time on the back end.
So, look I'm digging what I see
& I see you watching me
Maybe our bodies can blend
& I can moisturize your goatee

He was attracted and wanted some ass
So, to him this was all cool.
Nah, no spending nights
No cuddling
Limited interaction was the rule.
See I just need someone to come drop off some… dick
When I done had a rough day and
These people done made me sick
Bonus points of you come through
& Use your face as somewhere for me to sit.
You bring a smile to my face
Insides rearranged and displaced
You take me to this other worldly place
& All my stress is erased

Yet, eventually feelings crept in
Digging the conversations
No one else in the rotations
Texts and calls bringing elation
Aww fuck….
It's time for cessation.
Cause Now he on this shit like look
We either just friends,
or we relationship fucking.
Cause all this interaction
Got him acting like he want something
All this body bumping had him thinking he was thumping the strings to my heart
When in all actuality
I really meant what I said from the start
I wasn't looking for a counterpart
The last dude I had
This Nigga killed my heart.

All the the orgasms in the world
Couldn't even give it jumpstart.

They say women can't do friends with benefits
Because they get emotionally attached.
Maybe it was ON the masculinity in me
that the femininity in him latched
He thinking he in a love match
Meanwhile I'm enjoying what's in his drawls
& The pieces of my heart were detached
So, this… had to come to an end.
Cause without the benefits
I realize I didn't like him enough
To be just his friend.

Up

Confounded
Spatial inaccuracies
Worsened by disorientation
& Not knowing which way is up.
Close to drowning
Body needing air
Yet my disjointed mind,
Doesn't know whether or not to give a fuck.

Or maybe I do.
Don't wanna be the cause of another's grief
I don't want the ones I love,
or those that love me,
To feel, how it feels,
To carry what ails me,
Those I love I wish them to be
Infinitely happy
So, my seemingly effortless glide
Hides the struggles I hold inside.

Inadvertently confusing others,
Discomfort cleverly disguised by elation
No longer seeking cessation, through intoxication.
Dancing, laughing & talking
All temporary distractions from mental agitation.
(Deep sigh)

Confounded
Spatial inaccuracies
Worsened by disorientation
& Not knowing which way is up

& Sometimes not knowing,
Whether or not to give a fuck.
What I do know is I couldn't give up,
Even if I tried.
Every night I die
& Every morning the creator wakes me up
I'm given yet another chance
To fix & replace or repair my mess ups.
Granted infinite chances,

To try every different direction,
Til I find…my pathway up.

Partnership

In life you get bogged down
Sometimes in life you have to lift your head up to see
Not for comparison but to see what's in your vicinity.
Sometimes to see another's version of me
Sometimes to check out whether or not I'm feeling the me, that's me
Sometimes because I'm bored and I just want to see
Hell, sometimes a glimpse into another's life breaks the monotony

I have a life & goals
I checklist of what I need to do
Yet sometimes 4 eyes are better than two.
I like being alone
Yet Sometimes I like being alone, with you!
With you I can be alone & not be by myself
Knowing there's always someone there allows me to be share my best self.
I do what I do but when it time to put life of a shelf.
It's with you I wanna shut out the world with & enjoy my wealth.
It's with you I wanna show the cards I've been dealt
It's with you I want to trust writing my plans
It's with u I wanna show only things I show my man.
It's with you I wanna hash out plans to get these bands
Don't care about status or notoriety
I just want to share my thoughts through poetry
Be free
Travel the world
Have sex that's nasty
Enjoy my life & have a legacy to bequeath
Yet within my circle
I wonder Do they see me.
I mean the facets of me I want others to see
I keep Parts of me for you & me only
Partnership brings out the best in me.

Submission

Raised up in a Christian space
Taught the ways of a woman's "place"
Being soft spoken, demure,
Moving with style & grace.
Being a lady,
Not spreading my goodies all over the place.
Being a good girl,
Remaining chaste.

Some things, not taught with words,
But still shown.
Don't submit to any and every man,
& Whore-ish behavior not condoned
Every man doesn't deserve to be in your face.
Even less deserve to be blessed with the bliss of your holy space.

As I got older curiosity got the best of me.
Entertaining those that entertained me.
Quickly realized the power
Being a portal owner afforded me
Watching the things men would do just for a chance to get inside
Changed behavior,
Not so "quality" time,
Dropping gifts, money, even jewelry
So, in my inner space their rocket could glide

Because of this, true intentions,
they would usually hide
As if my discernment was misapplied.
Yet you, my dear, have passed the tests
& made it through the obstacle course.
Realizing no matched aggression,
Softness's essential…not force.
While others fought at the gate
You slipped right on in.
They fought, you won!
No competition.
Laughing, talking, & spending time
As my friend.

Quiet strength and cunning

Plus, a certain vulnerability
Got you into my world.
With Stick-to-itiveness & stability
Tranquility & affability
Intelligence, loyalty & trust
Giving Freedom…,
& not handcuffs.
Not only was my stargate opened
Faith…gave you the key
Through retention & dedicated exploration,
You learned my controls better than me.

Showed me reactions I've never seen.
Loving your version of our reality.
Trust……I'll follow wherever you lead. "Submission" even brought about changes
to my personality.
Yet, more like dominant and recessive
Instead of a slave mentality.
Bicep to tricep
OUR arm doesn't move without You & Me
The Yin to my Yang
Stronger is our combined chi.
Turns out you knew,
I'd fully submit to you, because you chose to submit to me.

Combustible Elements

Feeling you deep inside my core
Upper and lower palpitations…
When we part, we crave for more
Mental & Spiritual intoxication….
See, we are, co-creators
& what we create…hmmm
Look, Now, like an addiction,
it's you, I now crave
You've altered my frequency
& the pattern of my brainwaves

By the sight of you, I'm captivated
By your touch, I'm titillated
By your scent, I'm elevated
By your taste, I'm elated
By the feel of you
& Your skin on mine…
Your flesh within me, feels fated.

& By your absence…. I'm devastated
I know, I'm extra, …but you like how I do.
As contradictory as it sounds,
I sometimes need my space too.
So, I don't trip, when that desire comes from you.
&……When You have your cravings for me too.
Of calls, texts, vids, and pics, I have a Slew
Plus, you have a few items that sentimentality has given importance too.
Certain pieces that daily, brings me to the forefront of you mental queue.

A myriad of dimensions our love has brought me to.
Places only seen and explored,
When physically connected with you.
So many lack the fuel,
To arouse in others the fires within!
So many proclaim love
Yet what we have…. isn't common
& Because of insecurity & envy
Outside of the marriage bed
Society labels it a sin.

You are the oxygen to my heat
Sparks? Nah, you wanted a blaze
& To make all interactions before you obsolete,
Consumed by fire
We become the damn flames
Dancing around, snaking in and out,
As our bodies do the same.
& Fusion's singed my maiden name
However, spiritual and physical are not always
One and the same.

Now on display for all to see.
Your world & mine
Tossed, is my cloak of invisibility
Never in secret but privacy preferred
The dance of our fire, has others lost for words.
Our worlds adjacent,
Not previously connected, or fully entwined.
Yet this blaze, this fire,
Has stood the test of time
When stoked it's high
When left alone, even out in the cold
It doesn't die
Through death and rebirth
It's remains the same
When one of our hearts calls out
The other's soul hears it's name
When it's called the other comes
What We have is An Eternal flame
It burns without tending.
Fuck legal contracts,
Only a paradigm shift,
Could bring about its ending.

Disillusionment

Disillusion & confusion
Made me decide to chill
People out here fronting
like they out here looking for the real.
Making stupid ass decisions
& fucking up situations,
When they already had the real deal.
So now no seriousness
I just wanna play.
Now, I'm Out with that energy of Aunt Shirley's As We Lay.
We may do what we do but before morning we go out separate ways

Yet......The very next man I met.
Won't lie just wanted conversation,
wasn't even trying to get my ass wet.
I guess I knew not, what I beget
Maybe it was on my heart.
I guess God knew, what I Really wanted, from the start.
It was Calmness & familiarity
No flutters from the first look
& I Was feeling like fuck them niggas
I mean he looked like the rest,
But this lil dude here, had me shook
Was like the silver lining to storms in my mind
Or a Hail Mary pass from gods personal playbook
Whatever it was
Disillusionment now gone to waste
In my lap, this was placed
Believe me, I wasn't out looking for him.
My outlook on Love...that shit was grim.
It took a minute,
Didn't want to admit I was in it,
I wanted to fight it
Trying to be friends, not wanting to commit
Yet in my presence...
Hmm...the frequency he emits
Calmed my chaos so I'd willingly submit.
He said do and I did, without even thinking about it.

Then like most niggas here he comes with his own bullshit.
Everyone has a past, he came with a kid and woman trying to Reverse their split,

Even though she was the one who initiated it.
Yet the good, was so good, when the other shit came,
I wasn't daunted by it.
Not to mention, by that time I was mesmerized,
By the sausage between his thighs.
Man shit this Nigga had me taking……deep sighs
& I can admit it, I was a bit dickmatized.
Shit was so bad just him touching me with it
Caused the roll of my eyes.
Caused the feeling of a million mini explosions inside
On his chest, humph,
This Nigga rightfully wore his pride
Like there was an S on his chest
Not shown but implied
How he made me feel, shit
There was no use in trying to hide.
Chile don't get me started on the reaction when I would ride
He having regular sex.
My ass out here gliding with rainbows & butterflies in the skies….
Until I'm pulled back by my body convulsing
As I slide down the internal waves of ecstasy
& The waves are so strong, my back arches
As he's soaked by the waves spraying out of me.
I'm trying to catch my breath cause I'm now back in this reality.
Seeing my waters, excites him, so he flips me and digs deeply while hitting,
What I call my crazy button, repeatedly!

Right leg on his shoulder
His mouth on my left breast
Left leg around his waist
While I'm calling out the names of the books of the Bible
Cause his mama said, one of them suits him best.
Then he stops and starts suck on my clit,
Should've been nicknamed Satan
The way he sucked on my shit.
Wasn't he called the morning star
Cause I swear I saw the sunrise the way he sucked on it
Then he fucked me like his tongue was his dick
While licking my insides….
My soul, humph, I know this Nigga ingested my shit
Shit I called Emma and Gwen to tell them this lil dude right here, was it.

Damn, wait a minute, what was the name of this poem again
Yea, yea disillusionment.

Damn, I don't know if,
I'm more disillusioned now, than before
Or if he was god's way of telling me
I don't need to be disillusioned anymore.
I'm thinking I can deal with all his other shit
Some dudes be thinking their God's gift
My dude may actually be it.
Plus, according to the bible, the marriage bed is unsoiled
So, if we married, I can be his personal little whore.
All and all I'm glad those other niggas weren't shit
Cause this dude right here became the end of all my disillusionment.

Intimacy

Matters of love & intimacy…
Today, these things seem to be misunderstood
Giving money, gifts, trips & etc…
It's really…. all good
Then again, maybe it's not misunderstood.
Maybe it's just me.
Provision & protection isn't all that I need.
Those things are lovely but not what protection & and provision is to me.
Goal, not a gold-digger, yet to be in my life,
I expect a certain level of quality.
& those things are Required to see,
The soft nurturing side of me.

I need acceptance.
Are you cool with my unconventionality?
I have a praise kink,
& I NEED to hear that you're proud of me.
Can you be my teammate, yet knowing our only real competition is us?
Can you handle the intensity of my love,
As well as the severity of my lust?
I sometimes have this need to be alone.
Can you deal without thinking another has my attention or you've been dethroned?
Will you stick around, when I'm hard to deal with & my emotions get the best of me?
When I need reassurance?
Or a reminder of my sexy?
Cause when I truly feel safe,
You'll see parts you've never seen.
Things only shared with you, because they may be thought of as obscene.
Or only ever thought about because your energy meshed with mine, I mean.

I'm A true counterpart
While you pull, I'll push
My unflinching support
Unlocking new levels to my gush
I'll be the refuge you seek
When outside there's nothing but ambush.
When you need it, I'll be, the sun rays…
Peeking through the clouds of your mental haze.
Your biggest cheerleader,

There with you in your darkness
Yet continually pulling you into brighter days
The soft to your hard,
when you need something to hold.
My bosom your pillow as I wrap myself around you, to keep you warm,
Because the world outside can be so cold.
I'll be your solace,
Your sanctuary,
& My heart your abode.
To you being protected with blessings…
& Covered from, my prayer closet of old.

Yes, I watched my grandparents
That love was something awesome to see.
Something I desired to obtain for me.
Independent yet her femininity learned to match his masculinity
Imperfect, yet fitting together…. perfectly.
One thing my grandfather taught me
Sexuality isn't the true definition of intimacy
It's being Mentally, Emotionally and Physically bare for ONLY each other to see.

On Empty

Learning to fill the emptiness
That space that was left after you left.
Purging all the bad feelings and pain
Like ...an abscess
Heart now closed
No longer do you have egress
Revoked is your access
Not because of a loss of love
But more cause of regret

Feeling the love I had was one sided
To accommodate my life was divided.
Or compartmentalized
Not realizing what I'd chosen,
Was love bastardized.
How could I give rise to the feelings inside
When feelings I would hide.
You kept wanting me to let go.
Relax, release, just let emotions flow.
Yet I couldn't find comfort
Not in a situation where I couldn't see growth.

Not because of a future I couldn't see
I could literally see us on the porch chilling
The old you and me.
Even you as a grey-haired silver fox is sexy to me.
It was, because in the beginning your choice of words showed me,
your choice wasn't me.
Though, I stayed, stupidly,
for the physical ecstasy.
Those original words were never revised
At least not to me.
Actions are cool but I need to hear it.
Clarification.
A blending of the two.
So to me this connection was ultimately doomed.
Because love I had for you could bust out of any room,
yet it blinded me so I couldn't see if any love you had was true.

In my mind, you wanted the physical
You wanted what you could get

Don't care about title's yet
Is this even a relationship?
Or Friends with benefits?
I mean a couple of times I fell out of love
& Then right back in.
This shit we have is time tested, it's true.
As my man, husband, or my friend
My forever is you.

Soul ties are what I was told.
We have no "real" foundation,
so how come I have visions us growing old.
The foundation to me is that we friends.
Regardless of the love shit, friendship
& Respect wins out in the end.

Then again......
Here I am cleaning out and purging.
Cause I realize we've made a life
of not being really in each others lives.
Our paths aren't really connected
with or without lies
So It doesn't matter,
That I want to be with you.
I've learned despite all that
To thine self always be true.
So I purge now to detox myself
Of the cravings, of the flavor of you.
Shaking my head, to shake loose
Any left over mental residue.

You win.
I'm done.
No longer fighting to remain
I give up babe. The love is still there
I just no longer desire to be in your lane.
Take back the order of pleasure since it comes with a side of pain
Eventually one day if you can,
You can forget my name.
Or if you can't at the very least, never utter it again.

Timeline

You inside of me
Me in your world
Co-mingling uncontested
Wahla,.It's a girl

Life not birthed
Crushed self-worth
Leaving unattached verses
& Lifeless universes

Manifestation unmanifested
The untouchable affected
Mentally dejected
Emotions unprotected
Disembarkation selected

Eons have passed
Lives lived
Yet it's still yesterday
I can't deal
Time misconstrued
Cause we went separate ways
Pulled, Stretched & Propelled through
No matter the trajectory
All orbits lead to you.

Journey didn't end
Destiny not through
Can't break it
Can't end it
No bidding each other adieu
So fuck it lets face it.
Talk this shit through
I'll go first.
....Hey.... I love you.

In Memory Of

I've lost money, houses, family members, so friends, lovers & other babies too
Though my love, my hardest loss, was you.
I felt you growing in my womb.
I'd had miscarriages before
Yet Even Those experiences
Didn't prepare me for,
What was in store.
In my life and heart, for you, I'd made room.
I knew you were a girl
& In my mind's eye I could see
Those tight little Afro curls
& In your imagined face
I could see your dad's smile.
I'd even chosen your name…
You were my love child.

Your life cut short,
It Ended, way too soon
My life halted, as I was swept up in,
this emotional monsoon.

Your siblings, you didn't even get to see.
Daddy wasn't there
I was alone, it…. was only me.
The process quick….
Yet, felt like eternity
Won't lie, when you died…
With your last breath….
Went a larger than tiny piece of me
In that moment,…..I needed privacy
In that moment,…..I didn't even want to be

Yet I had to be strong,
As a mom, your siblings depend on me
& In a twisted turn of events
I walked away from your daddy
In his eyes, your tiny face haunted me.
I no longer wanted to be in this place
I couldn't stand being in his presence,
Or seeing his gorgeous face

When I saw him…
I couldn't do the things I needed to do
When I saw him…
My mind replayed the pain of what I'd been through.
When I saw him…
In my mind's eye I kept seeing you.
I think that diagnosis my counselor gave of PTSD may have actually been true.

Your remains placed in a planter
So, wherever I live there you will be.
You may be with the ancestors spiritually.
Yet, I couldn't deal with placing you,
My love, in a cemetery
So now as a plant
Your allowed to live on with me
I'm remembrance,
She's called by your name
& She lives on
In your memory.

Full Disclosure

Demure and quiet
Often got me underestimated
I was often hurt and taken advantage of by those I dated.
Until I stopped giving a fuck you see.
Please don't let the glasses fool you
In to misconstruing the power with in me.
Former foolishness made me learn to respect the Goddess energy within me.

That one your mama warned you about.
Mhm, that's me....

I came to taking complete joy in playing with a man's emotions.
& Took pride in securing a man's devotion
Guys out here struggling,
to hold in their jealousy.
Worrying bout if another,
Is touching my body.
Envious of other men that get a smile out of me.
Burning up inside,
just from me acting friendly.
After eating this puss &
giving me all he got to give
Face covered completely in my juices
This dude need a bib
Falling asleep with that Itis
Like he just ate a big ass plate of ribs.
Not even wanting me to go home.
Trying to hold me hostage at his crib.

Left, & didn't send a good night text
So he wondering if I'm creeping
While he in his bed tossing in turning
I'm in my king size peacefully sleeping.
His mama thinking I done, done voodoo!
At the prayer meeting,
His name to the list,
While they praying for his salvation.
All the while, I am his chosen Goddess.
There's a reason my name is
Torrential Bliss
This pussy got his brain stuck on reminisce

Not talking bout the song, but he on his Mary J shit
Tweaking to give my asshole another French kiss
& Loving my torrential rain be it cum or piss.

I'm the one grandma warned you about,
Mhm… that's me

Mama got him at Sunday service
Yet he tweaked out, thinking bout
praising….
and worshiping me
Not answering the altar call
He wants communion with me
Drinking my nectar and eating my body.
We from the south but I don't need spaghetti and things.
Me calls me his angel
Yet he rocks the red wings.
No need for deception
Full disclosure is what I bring
He was told what he was getting into
& He willingly does these things.

Mama & grandma out here hoping
it's just a fling.
But…To my bosom he wants to cling
 & This goddess energy got him out searching for rings
Souls ain't tied
They knotted up in this thing.
& I'm giving him the treatment of a King
That's why I'm on this in pedestal
as his Queen.

Curtain Call

This is goodbye... This is it.
This is the last performance.
So, I'm gonna make the best of it.
Not parting because a lack of love
Yet, sometimes mistakes
& Bad choices we make,
Bring about consequences & new paths,
We wouldn't normally take.

This new path takes me away from you.
Because we're adults
Even if we're not happy with the results
Because of responsibilities & obligations
We do what we gotta do.
So, for one last night you're gonna be all mine
I'm going all out
The only limit, Will be time
Imma show my ass
I gots-tah & leave you with memories sublime

As it gets closer to that time,
...excitement's building.
To preserve this memory...
Hmm...I'm thinking bout filming
Normally a brat
But tonight I'm not the one being tamed.
My aim is for the rest of your life,
To make your dick rise just a lil bit,
At the mention of my name.
I need you to salivate
As you remember my taste.
Don't care if you get married
Tonight, these memories,
Will forever be seared in place.
Of your top five, 1, 2 & 3 gotta move
'Cause Imma need all that space!

Attachments can be broken & sometimes bonds too
But real connections are never ending
Especially if it's true

So, you can be honorable
and I'll let you walk away.
Yet I'll enjoy the breeze at my house
On the seaside in your brain ev-ery-day!
Besides if it meant,
You'll find you way back, anyway

Surprised by the aggression brought
When we meet.
No time for words,
Directly to the bed & you throw up my feet.
Tongue kissing the portal,
Oh, you came ready to eat.
Not to be outdone,
My nails grip the back your head
Pushing your face deeper into my innerspace
You grip my cheeks as I grind on your face.
Flicks of your tongue takes it all away,
.... All gravity....
& Complete weightlessness
...Takes over me
I arrive & I arrive repeatedly,
Til' all fight was sucked out of me.
Flight too, as I'm consumed by your gentle savagery

So nah, tonight will not be a test of wills
Instead…
Dominance met…with complete receptivity.
Trust bestowed
& You claimed all that was given freely
Humph & I thought tonight was my turn to tame the beast.
Instead, I completely enveloped you,
In the softness of, my femininity.
What you gave… I received
Feeding your ego,
With the squeals and screams your thrusts brought out of me.
Even turned to the back so he could enter portal number 2
A lil bit of Our depravity coming through.
& My Openness to explore taboos
Not caring about tomorrow
You can do what you do.
Tonight, the interior & exterior of my star gates belong to you.
My back to your chest & I sit on your hips
Listening intently as directions flow from your lips.

As the night went on and the moon gave way to the sun.
Our chapter over, a new chapter's begun
With a hug & a kiss we went our separate ways.
Quietly we left.
No more words to impart.
knowing that forever we'll hold a special place
In each other's heart.

Relapse

I finished the 12-step program
I got myself clean.
I walked away prepared to even face the temptations I mean.
See there this certain elation that comes from overcoming something you thought
You'd always need
When your faced with your addiction
& You Maintain that control
& Not…succumbing to the affliction.

Situations when I was no longer in control
Situations where gratification was my only goal.
Situations where my future couldn't unfold
Situations where my addictions had me in a chokehold.
Situations had me Feeling like I'm prematurely…growing old…

Now, I'm good.
It's a re-introduction to me
Not just for the world
but for Me & you, both to see
I've come to accept and incorporate the newly found parts, within me
Giving myself grace
& Embracing myself softly
Realizing I am a star-seed
Realizing that no one compares to me
I've faced highs & lows & my own duality
My 4C locs connect to divinity
My toasted toffee skin covers me beautifully.
Moldable like clay,
Yet needing to be handled carefully!
Cause like C4 any mishandling can end destructively!

Then here you come like a firefighter
Seemingly trained to play with fire.
Armed with memories that are….
Relapse inspired
Handsomeness still admired
Still, feeling the flames of desire
Attempting to play with my mental
Knowing any physicality would backfire.
Yet, the feeling of giving a fuck, has expired.
One sided BS is the reason I withdrew

Say what you want.
Do what you do.
Admittedly, still addicted
Yet, I no longer Want you.

See you thought,
Like always, I'd eat the lies you bought
& Discernment would be fought
& Forgiveness given….
For treatment as an afterthought.
& I'd always given you at least,
One more shot.
Yet with any addiction.
At some point it has to stop.
Conquered or death
& Since I wasn't ready for my last breath,
I cleared the emotional debris.
After seeing things clearly,
I…chose… me!

Lost Key

The man I now see
Caused the man conjured in my imagination
To cease...to be.
The lies, neglect and sometimes drama
Took the rose-colored glasses off me.
So, I sit back, taking you,
The man in front of me,
In, fully

No longer fooled by your lies of omission
Now realizing our relationship has within it
Different levels of decomposition.
Feeling foolish for my submission
No longer your loyal slave
Truth...was my manumission.
No more....
Being love starved into malnutrition.

I needed your love
I needed to be true
I needed to only be yours
I only needed you.
Emotions so deep
Scuba gear's needed to dive in
Yet the dam works so well
Seems you forgot the size of the lake within

Breastfed you commitment
You licked loyalty off my clit
Imbibed each other's soul
Connection on my end was thick
But...I guess mine, didn't stick
Cause Fidelity flew out the window
As she sat on your dick.

Her elation's now laughing, walking & talking, As your obligation
Yet now, you wanna talk relation - ship,
Friendship, & Respect, Ha, Boy please!
With that mess, You & your BM can miss me!
& To my heart, baby
Nah, you no longer hold the key.

Competition

I don't know what made you decide to try me
I chill
Girl!! I Don't mess with nobody.
Only thing I can think of is your insecurity
I'm thinking Oh my
what a tangled web she's weaved
I'm amused cause I know her,
but she doesn't know me
I'm the reason for the induction of her jealousy
Lil mama came through with face, the hair,
The nails, booty, and shoes!
Not even noticing that I'm sitting back in the gap too.
Chilling with my people
Ya know, we're doing what we do.
I'm smiling to myself because she thinks she is bringing pressure too.

Won't lie Lil mama looking fly
I can't even lie
I ought to boost her ego a lil bit
& let my dog, Rydell, go tell her Hi!

I left him alone years ago
Yet I'm still the apple of his eye.
Poor thing she don't even know
While he's with her, throughout his mind I go
I can't help, the impression that I leave
I can't help, your man fantasizing about me
I can't help, what you think is evidence of infidelity
Is nothing more than simple relational debris
Can't help your relationship is haunted by my memory
When it comes to him
He's your man
You simply can't compete with me
You, my dear are with this man,
Cause, I chose not to be.

Unseen

I stand here before you
& I'm still not seen.
Yet you wonder
Why I won't let our bodies convene.
Broken communication
Misconstrued connotation
Although I see everything you wish you said
Reading body language & facial expressions
Maybe a lost art but it's not dead
Yet your body language doesn't match the words flowing out your head.
I'm told to trust what you say
& Not trust what I see.
So, I'm supposed to trust you,
Over my own understanding?
My grandpa taught me that actions are where you find true meaning.

I stand here before you and I'm still not seen.
My silence worn, like a cloak of invisibility I mean.
I spend my time trying to understand & make sure I'm understood
Is what I do, & did, well before you.
Yet, asking for clarity is wrong too.
Asking you to decipher
What my senses are telling me is untrue.
& I'm told focusing on negativity, is what I do.
Yet the world isn't all positive
It's a mixture of good and bad
Yet asking simple questions makes you mad.
I want to understand why you do, what you do
Yet I explain my actions but the words are lost on you.
Mainly because I'm not something you pay attention to.

I stand here before you and
I'm still not seen
Well unless it's for sexual purposes I mean.
We've gone on for so long
Because of what I believed.
You were my husband, so it was my duty, to please.
Even if I didn't want to,
Even if it wasn't on my mind.
Even if I'm not turned on

Hell, I didn't have to even be awake sometimes.
Although it was bad if I was awake
and fell asleep
Yet it's cool, if I was sleep
and only awakened after you entered me.

I stand here before you
& I'm still not seen
Most of the intimacy I feel
Flows from my brain to my fingertips
To appear on my screen.
When you tell me about our passion, I don't know what you mean.
An overheard conversation with you and your friend in year 3
is when passion left me.
It returned in spurts but never fully.
If I'm honest it was that split that started us growing separately.
I am, who I am, and you still can't see
Although I have a bit more of your attention
Because I refuse to submit even sexually.

Numb

Peaceful coasting
Desires dormant
No matter who's present,
Encased in solitude
Lack of shock
No real reaction to attitudes
Not even caring about others being rude
Feeling the breeze go through my hair
The look of not having a care.

Stuck between come and go
Destination?
....I don't even Know.
To be honest
I don't even really care.
I guess the real me is somewhere in there
Maybe one day she'll resurface
When she does maybe she will share.

Right now on autopilot
& comfortably numb.
I'm mildly amused that those I gave everything too
Now ok with crumbs
I wonder if my former intensity
Was too much
& they welcome this shadow of me.
Oh well.
Doesn't matter anyway &
I can give me, partially
Gladly.

Alone

We had a time, and it was fun.
Getting to know each other
Watching the years go and come.
Remembering the time just being in your company my heart would beat
Like a bass drum
Who…. would have known the outcome
My love for you was as deep as can be
At times I believe, I loved you more than me
Feeling your touch gave me 9 different levels of happy
You brought friendship, pleasure, passion and ecstasy more importantly you
stimulated me mentally

Never imagined I would one day feel this way
Never imagined I would one day have these words to say
Never imagined my welcome I'd outstay
Watching this illusion of a relationship crumble and decay.
Never did I imagine one day, I would walk away.

So, in love I watched the changes In you
So, I love I let you do what you do
So, in love I continue to show up….
& with a broken heart too
So, in love I couldn't imagine life without you

I would lie in the dark not wanting to see the light
I would lie in the dark, fuck fight or flight
I would lie in dark tears in my ears
 and sad lyrics I'd recite
I would lie in the dark praying love would be finite
I would lie in the dark hoping for perpetual night

Yet like always the morning did come
and the sun did arise
I'm a big girl
& the truth was surmised
Eventually able to go cold turkey on the addiction of having you inside.
Eventually seeing some of my choices…
Were probably unwise
Eventually, I acted my age & swallowed my pride.
Eventually threw on my heels & adjusted my stride

Love isn't finite,Wwhen it's true
Yet loving someone doesn't require attachment or tethering to
So fully in love, I walked away from you
Believing if it was meant to be
Love never really dies
And somehow
Some way,
Someday,
Will return to me.
Yet, Being alone….
Hardest shit I ever had to do.
Yet, I became the center of my innerverse
Not you
A friend once told me sometimes you have to leave the one you love
To find the one that loves you.

Why am I here?

Why am I here?
I didn't seek you out
You chased me.
Yet our intentions from the beginning
We're different, I see.
I was alone. Not lonely.
U came, gave attention & time

Yet there's no growth

Why am I here?
Do you keep me around, so you feel adored?
So, when your missed shots elsewhere,
start to add up
Me. Ur biggest cheerleader,
Makes you feel like you scored?
Does Me being in love with You
Make you feel less than a man-whore?
Fantasies, it seems built, only, in my mind
Foundations of falsehoods, galore.
Do you ever wonder If the truth came out, would it be you, I deplore?
Would I look upon our memories as an eyesore?

Why am I here?
It's not me, with whom,
you wanna love on & grow
Building empires & legacies, to which
You'll be a no show
No need for apologies
Given for just show
There's not even anger, for what I now know
Just wish my eyes were always open
So I could've let go.
No more hiding feelings,
& holding out for hope
No new last name you will ever bestow

Why am I here?

Just to feed your ego?
Instead of a love pill
You fed me a placebo
Just like that. Hook, line & sinker
I was all in.
Like that forbidden apple
I willing took part in my own sin
I'd tell myself never again
Yet, stupidly I loved you…past the end.
You were the fire
& I unsuccessfully… tried to play fireman
No quitter but I'm tired
I just want to see the end
Your turn for a response.
I need an answer!
Why am I here again?

ReBirth

Your responses dance,
On the fine line of manipulation.
Yet unmatched is the mental stimulation
Your presence creates physical temptations as
Your fingertips play melodic tunes in my hair.
Your touch creates orgasmic elation
So enveloped in you, I want to breathe your air.

I'm filled with angst from your sticky words
Stuck in my brain
I want to disappear, yet here, I still remain
On autopilot....my heart's been trained
Replaying our times together over
....and over again
My lips now curl at the mention of your name.

A simple "Hi".... & I smile, I'm back the zone
Emotions swell from memories of your baritone
Demeanor calm, but energy overgrown
I want you, I'm smitten, Tú Eres mi Corazón

Intensity's telling me to leave,
I'm cool with being alone
Wouldn't matter, if I did
Your hands are now my heart's home.
Don't want to be foolish
Too soon to feel this way
My cerulean blue lost in your shades of grey
Listening to Aunt Shirley talk about "As we Lay" ...
Traumatized by the trail of fire left by your lips
My landscape barren,
You're my personal apocalypse
Our fire's so intense I could not breathe
Trembling as I shake off the ashes of our ecstasy
Through our passions I've been transformed
Fight, not flight has me now reborn.

Right Person/Wrong Time

When it's worth it,
Never give up is my motto.
I was struck & It came to mind
From the moment you said Hello.
Didn't understand why, at the time.
I'd given up on men,
So, The Creator gave me a glimpse
of the end of the line.
Not death but when it's time,
for the Love inside me to shine.
I don't think,
I know. I was destined to be yours
& you to be mine.
Intellect piqued & You digging my vibe
Quiet but humorous &
I'm thinking damn you're fine
Yet, like young habitual line steppers
We repeatedly crossed that line.
Didn't understand then,
right person/ wrong time.
.

Your foreign approach disarmed me.
Addictive to me was your technique.
Feeling accepted, acknowledged
emotionally safe, listened to, & heard
The line between friendship and more became blurred.
I went from assertive, to submissive & meek
You even sparked the release
of my inner freak.
I Didn't know she existed so that was one hell of a meet & greet.
Your structure, self-control
& Demeanor, calms me.
Bar raised; mind blown
My heart, now a place,
Your's could call home
No forethought
Naturally flowing together, off the dome
Yet this was supposed to be just a snippet
Not something I could keep as mine
Still didn't understand,
Right person/wrong time.

We went our separate ways
& thought it was the end.
You, with other women
& Me with other men
Various choices & situations
 we put ourselves in
Yet, While apart, in my head & dreams,
you remained
Even while with others,
lessons you inadvertently taught…retained
& Frustration from others,
From Their lack of being trained
The fire that we created
Left uncontrolled & untamed
Desire refusing to be quenched without mentally calling your name.
Bringing forth a yearning to nurture you
& Lay my head on your chest
Hearing your rhythmic breaths
Entices my insomnia to succumb to rest
Maturity, Growth & experiences has me at peace
Embracing where I am,
while looking forward to the end of the line.
I now understand,
Right person/wrong time.

Limerence

A simple touch reaffirms our connection
Sharing previously unseen parts of my reality.
Yet, You're always in my head,
So, it's more like introspection.
Stomach caresses,
Not inherently sexual…simple affection
There's meaning behind it
& reassured is how I feel.
& Despite life and everything thing else
What I know is…this right here, is real.
Your presence brings comfort
& familiarity too.
& you replenish my energy
So, I can do what I do.
Right now though,
I just need to soak up you.
Cause…. I've missed you.

I readjust
& Your hand transitions,
from my stomach to my back.
Leaving trails of fire on my skin
Mmm.., Heart arresting like cardiac
No moan escaped. Not even a sigh
Yet you interpret my silence
While looking in my eyes
Then, reading the shivers on my skin
As you uncase my thighs
I'm putty & your hands I'm in.
Inner sanctum stretched,
to accommodate Your girth.
You slow my pace, as my composure drops
& my desires become overt.

When we are apart…
limerence hidden by calm placidity
Our communication giving this obsession validity
It's seems my very physical orgasms
to your mental stimulation
We're just an elaborate form of manifestation.
& tonight is the very real result of my imagination.
& varying depths of deep are dug in various places without cessation.

You're weaving words in my mind
With your perfect dictation
Though my ankles covered your ears,
It didn't stop you from hearing our tones
my squeals and your moans forming a musical collaboration.
Or feeling my insides gripping you as my eyes rolled & my body shook in
celebration.
Damn,.I've missed you.

You'll never be the same!

I am the only person that can trip up me
Not to put anyone one down
I have love for my friends, fans and devotees.
Yet, It's not narcissistic
to love oneself intrinsically
Even in the throes of passion
Hell, I'm turned on by own energy
I'm turned on by how turned on he is wanting me
Hell, it's my energy that's making him
Feel temporarily complete
When I'm away
It's for me, that he tweaks
I can't even be mad. I understand.
Cause I love me some me!

Poetic Process

I am the art in author
A blended balance of masculine & feminine
The receptive nature in me Is fluid
& takes in the environment that I'm in
Inspiration like ovulation
Ideological Flirtation
Cogitative temptation
Lyrical infatuation
Kisses give way to
Bouncin....
Grinding....
& Mental gyration
The mental expansion
The building of poetic elation...
The..
The culmination
Becomes fertilization
When ink hits paper
& I ejaculate emotions
from the tip of my pen.
& Sometimes when My Muse gets me going.
Whew!
I wanna write again and again!
Man (sigh)
sometimes the ejaculation doesn't bring about the end.
The rush to find more paper
But my fingers are covered in blue or black ink
Ohhhh
My face flushes
With musings ranging from soft porn to kink
& (deep sigh)
I've even thought about joining with others
Ya know groupthink...
Shit.
Hmm...relaxation calms
& The cerebral expansion shrinks
In the end the poetry
My poems
My anthology
Are the results of my high jinx

Apologies

Riding with him
His hands on my thigh
I'm playing coy
But, but this edible just kicked in
So, I'm feeling high
He thinks I'm mad
He was caught in his lie
Not even realizing
I'm always on his side
He's not on my level
Cause he doesn't drink or get high
I wonder if he knows
I'm forever his friend
That ride or die.
& He will always get that respect
In the streets…United
When alone, situations we dissect

I see what others see
I don't trip,
That's their opinion.
It doesn't apply to me
All I ask you for is your honesty
Respect my mind enough
To be real with me
Don't take away my choice
Give me the truth, and the opportunity

What happened has happened
Situation is done
Commotion died down
Dust settled
See…. I didn't run.
I'm bout a mental connection
Cause emotions go and they come.
That anger you see in me is your guilt
A projection
I'm still standing here
You're my selection
I let you get all out.

Ignoring the urge to kiss you in the mouth.
Your apologies have me wanting
to show you, my affection
In my voice, I know you hear the inflection
This vibe I'm trying to take
In another direction
You're whiggin a lil bit
Thinking bout rejection,
Calm down, I'm thinking,
Fuck all that. I need an injection,
Below the midsection
Front or back, I don't care
You make the selection
Seriously though, appreciate you giving my feelings protection
Right now though babe, I need your erection.

Art Show

Upcoming art show,
And...The featured artist is me.
Showing off my creations, my art, & my personality.
Excited, because a featured artist, isn't something everyone gets to be.
Everyone isn't picked by the curator,
To come out of obscurity.
Most are left to their own devices
Some with talent, their chances, squandered by their own vices.
Seen some of the chosen crack under pressure
So,, the actual show they never get to see.
Then some reach a level of fame,
That they come to require security.
That's not really an aspiration
Yet, I don't know if that's what's meant to be.
I thought my role was a supporting player.
Apart of another's show, like an Emcee

Never thought all eyes would be on me.
I was satisfied helping others
be all they could be.
Never dreamed my role-playing support cast
Was simply preparation for when the spotlight was on me.
Now it's my turn &
I'm Confused about what the world wants to see.
Should I make myself more digestible?
Will they really like me?
I mean, what is it that they're really coming to see?
Are they really interested in getting to know me? Really?
Is this a waste of time and no one will come to see?
Or is this is just stage fright coupled with insecurity?

My creations...
Are fractal reflections of my own energy.
My poetry is simply versions of emotions written cleverly.
My paintings are visual representations of my dreams.
2D versions of the dimensions I traverse in my personal
InnerVerse, I mean.
Never realizing what the public has come to see.

Not diminishing my other art.
It was the self-portrait…. Mee,
Showing the world, the way I see me.
No outside influences, no assistance,
No suppressing certain parts
I'm told the blending and brush stokes
Are an indicator of my smarts
No restrictions
Giving full frontal
Not even hiding my heart.
Showing my care
My perversions
Even my kinky
My preferences, desires,
& the space that I need…
So, I can showcase the full me.
Lights turned dim
So, the public can take in my full glow.
The flames sometimes seem scary or wild,
yet are contained like the dance of the flambeaux
My Forever said,
Do. Not. Censor. Me!
& The curator sent me to give a full show.
Ok so, here I go!

Self Portrait (Art Show Pt. 2)

The streaks of grey in my hair.
Simply a hint of the wisdom that lives within me
& The stretch marks showcase…my resiliency.
The scars show the strength to mend
& overcome whatever's thrown at me.
Plus I'm told they add character to what you see.
My breasts, though still magnificent,
no longer have their former swell.
However, they still do one of their jobs.
They grab attention & compel.
My FUPA is a remnant of what used to be
It was like A kangaroo pouch to grow and nourish my babies.
Going lower brings you to a water filled oasis.
A handful of ass, & piercings in interesting places.
Yet…. An additional fee required,
To enter those intimate spaces!
Then there are my tattoos.
Each has its own meaning.
Used them so I can outwardly see,
& Heal my internal pain.
Yet I'm told sometimes booze or THC does the same
All of that before the exhibit even enters my brain
You might want a drink before you enter.
To the right, you'll see the champagne.
Cause it's about to get deep. & deeply personal to me.
My brain has always held more weight,
than my sexuality.

I was chosen…My Daddy wanted me.
A vehicle for him to love my mama through.
Yet, he took a bullet to the head,
when I was only 2.
An ex, took his life rather than seeing him with another.
My father figure then became my uncle, his lil brother.
Then when I was 11, a bullet to the head took him away from me too.
You think that's a lot but that's not even all I went through.
From abuse to rape, The story's insane
I'm not a victim or survivor,
I don't identify with those names.
I couldn't have made it this far

If that pain was not overcame.

I came to think…
From love I had to stay estranged.
It seemed when I loved hard, openly & unashamed.
From Love to Abandonment the narrative changed.
I learned respect & true friendship is what remains the end.
If I ever took another's name.
He would first have to be my friend

Now on my journey, on others, at times
I inflicted pain of my own
Like the crazy…of me, pistol whipping a nigga for playing with child &
disrespecting my throne.
Yet, I caused no harm,
unless harm was done to me.
Well, nah I just took it.
Though, he crossed the line fucking with my baby.
Like TLC, The Cool & Sexy, followed my Crazy.

I Am Triumph & my past does not define me.
See the bloodstains in my past are just stories behind the colors, blended to makeup
my beauty.
The curator does not give us things, with which we cannot deal.
Stopping only prolongs,
you have to continue through, in order to heal.
I experienced the pure love of a big brother.
& He was my protector too.
Yet my grandfather did the things a dad was supposed to do.
I've seen variations of maternal or feminine love too.
Some I wanted to emulate.
Others doing shit, I would never do.

Then there is some people's favorite part.
Mhm what some of y'all really came to see.
How I see, my own sexuality.
Y'all see I'm quiet with the pretty face & glasses,
So I got to be a freak.
Well, I'm normally spoiled and vanilla asf.
I'm like pillow princess that loves to get pleased.
Any scars on my legs come from tattoos
And not bruised knees.
That's not to say I haven't gotten down and dirty before
Mental connection turned me into My Forever's personal little whore.

Riding, squatting, squirting on the dick.
Giving out palpitations,
Like a blood pressure cuff with it.
Knees were not bruised
Because a pillow was placed for the queen's knees to sit.
When fed. I ate, (no hands) & swallowed,
Shit, Because I was taught, it was unladylike to spit.
Maybe I should explain the name
Torrential Bliss
He's blessed with my Bliss
& My orgasms come with the flow of torrents.
All of this…sums up the portrait, standing before you.

In Life We must go through & digest it all
Like a full meal.
Spotlight not given where distraction
& Avoidance are chosen as ideals.
Yet I got my feature and…
I'm a blessing, because of surviving my ordeals.
The depth of my pain,
Has given me the biggest heart.
I love all of my creations!
I however … I know I am….
My own best damn work of art!

Thank you!

Thank you for taking the time to peruse my Poetic Innerverse
I hope you enjoyed my poetry!

Checkout my websites
www.BlissJones.com
www.rigellemedia.org
www.tiktok.com/@torrential_bliss
& Follow me on social media
www.facebook.com/blissjonesauthor
www.intagram.com/torriential_bliss

Please look out for the third book in The Innerverse Series
The Afrodesia Realm
and other upcoming titles from Rigelle Media Group.